Greening Your Finances

A Guide to Sustainable Personal Money Management

Table of Contents

Chapter 1. Introduction

In today's world, where sustainability is no longer a choice but a necessity, this Special Report, "Greening Your Finances: A Guide to Sustainable Personal Money Management", brings a fresh perspective to your fiscal affairs. Navigate through your financial dealings with a renewed consciousness, as this guide shows you how making eco-friendly choices can boost your savings and your planet simultaneously! Not only will you learn about the nuts and bolts of green finance but also see how taking small steps can contribute to a big impact. Cheerful, inspiring, yet astoundingly simple, this report will make you see your finances and investment selections in a new light. Prepare to embark upon a deliciously green journey towards a financially secure, and environmentally friendly life! So, are you ready to infuse a dash of green into your personal assets? This is not just another report, it's your bridge to a sustainable future. Let's make your money talk green!

Chapter 2. Understanding Green Personal Finance: A Primer

Green finance, a concept rapidly gaining traction, represents an intersection of finance and sustainability that you, as an individual, can implement in your personal money management practices. However, to do so effectively, having a firm understanding of its fundamentals is critical. This section aims to break down the concept of green personal finance, its importance, the potential benefits, and how to get started on your journey to sustainable finance.

2.1. The Basics: What is Green Personal Finance?

Green personal finance - alternatively referred to as sustainable, ethical, or responsible personal finance - is a holistic approach to managing your money that takes into account financial returns as well as the environmental, social, and ethical impacts of your financial decisions.

Broadly, green personal finance encompasses everything from the choices you make about how to save and invest your money, to the manner in which you spend it, to the financial institutions you choose to trust with your finances. In moving this direction, you're not just looking at your financial health and the potential for returns but also considering how your fiscal actions influence the world around you.

2.2. Why Green Personal Finance Matters?

Beyond potentially growing your finances and savings, adopting green personal finance strategies can have a significant impact on our planet and society.

1. Environmental Pros: The more individuals choose to invest in environmentally-friendly activities, the more resources can be devoted to tackling climate change, preserving biodiversity, and promoting sustainable practices.

2. Social Benefits: By focusing investments and spending in line with ethical principles, green personal finance can also contribute to poverty reduction, improved labor conditions, and fair-trade practices.

3. Potential for Improved Returns: Strong sustainability credentials are increasingly linked with strong financial performance. Businesses that act responsibly tend to experience fewer costly incidents, be better positioned to adapt to new regulations, and often have more loyal customers – all of which could potentially drive higher returns.

2.3. How Do I Recognize Green Financial Choices?

Recognizing green financial options can initially be challenging. However, keeping in mind the following points may assist:

1. Engage with Green Financial Institutions: Some banks and credit unions have made it their mission to drive positive environmental and social impact through their financial services. Research your current bank's practices or consider a switch to a green-focused institution.

2. Invest in Green Funds: Investment funds that focus on sustainably-driven companies often indicate this alignment clearly, with phrases such as "Environment, Social and Governance (ESG)", "Sustainable" or "Impact" often used in the fund name or description.

3. Green Spending: Using your spending power to support businesses that emphasize sustainability can contribute to the green economy.

2.4. Embracing Green Personal Finance: Where do I Start?

1. Green Banking: Consider starting your green personal finance journey by scrutinizing where you bank. Do they invest in fossil fuels or controversial industries? Or do they support renewable energy, sustainable development goals, and socially responsible businesses?

2. Green Investments: ECO-ETFs, Green bonds, Socially Responsible Investments (SRIs), and Community Investment Notes are all investment opportunities with a positive environmental or social impact.

3. Conscious Consumption: Always prioritize sustainable and ethical businesses wherever possible. Look for businesses with certifications (like Fair Trade or B Corp) and public commitments to sustainability.

4. Get Informed: There are plenty of resources available to help you grow your understanding of sustainable personal finance. Non-profits, blogs, podcasts, and books dedicated to this topic can be instrumental in your journey.

While green personal finance may initially seem like a labyrinth, armed with a proper understanding, it becomes a manageable path to navigate. The key is to understand that the impacts go beyond your personal ledger and extend outwards towards societal and planetary benefits. Small changes you incorporate today can collectively lead to a very significant impact. Green personal finance is not just a trend, but a sustainable and ethical way towards future financial security.

Chapter 3. Decoding the Relationship between Your Money and the Environment

Understanding the symbiotic relationship between your financial behaviors and the environment provides the foundation upon which you can establish a more sustainable personal money management approach. The importance that your monetary decisions have on planet Earth cannot be overstated. Each choice invites consequences that reverberate far beyond your personal balance sheet, ricocheting throughout this interconnected world in ways that are often invisible to the naked eye.

3.1. The Butterfly Effect of Financial Decisions

Just as the proverbial flap of a butterfly's wings can set off a cascade of weather changes, your everyday financial choices can trigger a chain of actions that impact the environment, often with lasting consequences. Whether it's the decision to get that daily takeaway coffee, or a hefty investment in the stock market, these humble choices cumulate into a large footprint.

However, shifting these same decisions through a green lens can set off a positive butterfly effect - conserving resources, minimizing waste, encouraging sustainable practices, and supporting companies that prioritize environmental responsibility.

3.2. Revisiting Your Spending Habits

Consider this: Every dollar you spend is a vote cast for a certain type of world. When you purchase products or services, you directly support the resources used, the production methods employed, and the business practices upheld.

Thus, by consciously choosing to purchase eco-friendly products, you contribute to the demand for green alternatives. Companies, noticing this shift in demand, may pivot to desired sustainable practices, ultimately benefiting the environment. If practiced collectively, this change in consumer behavior can significantly drive market trends towards sustainable options.

3.3. Banking and Environment

Traditional banks invest your money, often in large sectors such as fossil fuels that have a massive carbon footprint. Green banking, on the other hand, invests in eco-friendly ventures. By switching to banks offering green banking options, you promote responsible lending and foster sustainable business growth.

Moreover, digital banking over physical branches can dramatically reduce your carbon footprint by saving paper and minimizing commutation.

3.4. Investing in a Green Future

Your investments are potent tools to shape the future. When you invest in green funds or sustainable stocks, you're directly funding companies adhering to environmental guidelines, responsible raw material sourcing, waste management, and opting for renewable energy.

Contrarily, investing in non-environmental-friendly companies can inadvertently contribute to planetary damage. Therefore, integrating ESG (Environmental, Social, and Governance) factors into your investment decisions is crucial.

3.5. Exploring Green Insurance

Insurance investments can also sway the balance towards sustainability. Climate insurance, especially, contributes towards the reduction of risks associated with climate change. Investments in such insurance firms are an affirmation of your support towards climate resilience efforts.

Additionally, some insurance companies are taking strides in sustainability by investing their premiums into environmentally-friendly sectors.

3.6. The Impact of Taxes and Subsidies

Government policies, including taxes and subsidies, influence environmental impacts. Tax benefits on electric vehicles and solar panels, subsidies for sustainable farming, and the like, can intensify or mitigate environmental effects. Being aware of these policies can help direct your financial choices more sustainably.

3.7. Pension Plans and Environment

Your pension fund does not need to sit idle. By choosing a green pension plan, your retirement savings can be invested in ethical funds, promoting low carbon technologies, renewable energy, and supporting businesses with strong sustainability goals.

In conclusion, the connection between your money and the environment is far-reaching and profound. Establishing a sustainable personal money management mechanism means more than just switching to eco-friendly consumption practices; it embraces a broader understanding of weaving sustainability into your financial behaviors. Through informed decisions, and by reinforcing positive actions and strategies, we can contribute to a shift towards a sustainable economy while climbing towards personal financial success. What we need to always remember is that with each financial decision, we have an opportunity to vote for the world we want to live.

Chapter 4. Eco-friendly Banking: The Green Giants of the Financial World

The financial sector has seen significant changes over the years, including the rise of eco-friendly institutions. Studies suggest that banks and other financial institutions that align themselves with the principles of sustainability are more attuned to the present and future needs of their customers and the planet.

Let's delve into the fascinating world of environmentally friendly banking, exploring the strides and innovations made by financial institutions eager to invest in, and protect, our planet.

4.1. Banks and Their Environmental Footprints

Banks, like other major corporate entities, have environmental footprints. The operations, including office facilities, staff commutes, business travels, and massive amounts of paper usage for statements, forms and legal documents, contribute to the carbon footprint of these institutions.

Many banks are increasingly aware of the significance of these environmental impacts. They have begun implementing practices such as paperless banking, energy-efficient branches, green buildings, and supporting renewable energy projects, all aimed at reducing their carbon footprint.

4.2. The Rise of Green Banks

Green banks, also identified as green finance, are banks that focus not just on earning profit, but also on the impact their investments and lending practices have on the environment. They follow environmentally friendly operations and engage in lending whereby potential borrowers' environmental strategies and impacts are considered.

Specifically, green banks invest in environmentally friendly businesses. This can be a company focused on renewable energy resources like solar farms or wind energy projects, or a business committed to building products using recycled materials. Through their investments, green banks are affecting positive change towards a sustainable future.

4.3. The Benefits of Eco-Friendly Banking

There are several key merits of eco-friendly banking. Primarily, it contributes to a healthier environment by promoting renewable energy projects and sustainable businesses. Such initiatives lead to reduced reliance on fossil fuels and less pollution.

Secondly, green banking can also be seen as a risk mitigation strategy. By considering environmental impact in investment decisions, banks can avoid businesses likely to be affected by climate-related risks, thereby protecting their investments.

Additionally, green banking appeals to a growing demographic of environmentally conscious consumers, intrigued by financial institutions that align with their values. This increasing customer base can lead to more profits and a better reputation for the bank.

4.4. Case Studies: Leading Green Giants

There's no better way to comprehend the impact of eco-friendly banking than by examining real-world examples. Here are some global players making waves in sustainable finance:

ING: Dutch banking giant ING takes a strong stance on sustainability, integrating it into its business strategy. It provides green loans, sustainable investments, and innovative products like the 'Green Bond'. They also use an extensive risk evaluation to ensure the green credentials of their credits.

Triodos Bank: Known as one of the world's most sustainable banks, Triodos, a European bank, finances projects with social, environmental, and cultural value. Plus, it practices complete transparency in sharing where every Euro is invested, helping customers see the direct impact of their money.

Amalgamated Bank: An American bank, Amalgamated, is fully committed to socially responsible banking. From supporting affordable housing projects to providing substantial funding for renewable energy, this institution utilizes money as a force for positive social, cultural, and environmental change.

4.5. Challenges & Future of Green Banking

The journey towards 'being green' is not without challenges. Banks face issues like lack of awareness among customers, need for advanced technology, government regulations, and the lack of expertise in estimating risks associated with green projects. Efforts are being made to overcome these hurdles by enhancing customer awareness on green banking, improving governance, and providing training to bank personnel.

As awareness grows and with more innovations in technology, the concept of green banking will likely mature and proliferate further. Banks will be more concerned about 'greening' their portfolios and offering more eco-friendly products and services. Green banking will not just be an option but will become the norm.

In this journey towards sustainable financial practices, through eco-friendly choices, you become participants and enablers of this beneficial change. The credibility of eco-friendly banks is on an upward trend. It's not just about your money anymore - it's about the alignment of your financial practices with positive environmental impacts.

When you choose to align with a green bank, you're not just choosing better services and products - you're playing your part in healing our planet and promoting a healthier and safer environment for generations yet to come.

Chapter 5. Smart Green Investments: Making Your Money Work for the Planet

Investing in sustainable and responsible financial opportunities not only offers the potential for substantial income growth, but it also allows you to positively contribute to a world grappling with climate change. Your investments can help fund projects and companies actively working towards reducing their carbon footprint, embracing renewable energy, and promoting sustainability.

5.1. The What and Why of Green Investments

Green investments are, at their core, any kind of investment made in projects or companies that are committed to conserving natural resources, producing and discovering renewable energy sources, and implementing environmentally friendly practices. Common green investments include green bonds, solar and wind energy companies, and ETFs that specifically focus on socially responsible investing.

Green investing is becoming increasingly popular for several reasons. First, sustainable investing is not just good for the planet, but good for your wallet as well. A study by MSCI showed that companies with strong ESG (Environmental, Social, and Governance) practices demonstrated a lower cost of capital and lower volatility than companies without such practices.

In addition, sustainability-focused businesses are often better positioned to deal with potential crises such as environmental disasters or stricter environmental regulations. Therefore, investing in these businesses can potentially result in less investment risk in the long term.

Finally, green investing allows you to support companies that align with your personal values. With green investing, you can make a positive impact on the world while potentially earning profits.

5.2. Decoding Green Bonds

A key component of green investing, green bonds are fixed-income securities that are designed specifically to fund projects that have positive environmental benefits. The proceeds from these bonds go towards projects that combat climate change - such as renewable energy, energy efficiency, green transport, and water conservation projects.

Green bonds offer a dependable return on investment and have seen exceptional growth over the past years. For instance, according to the Climate Bonds Initiative, the total issuance of labelled green bonds reached $269.5 billion worldwide in 2020. By investing in green bonds, you contribute to a sustainable global economy while receiving a stable income.

5.3. The Power of Solar and Wind Energy

Solar and wind energy are two of the most promising sectors within green investing. Increasing concerns over air pollution and climate change, paired with technological advances, have made renewable energy a viable investment.

Investing in companies that produce wind and solar energy, manufacture parts for these industries, or assist in their distribution and implementation has the potential to offer significant returns. As governments around the globe continue to impose more restrictions on fossil fuel usage while offering incentives for renewable energy, the outlook for solar and wind energy investments looks promising.

5.4. Exchange-Traded Funds (ETFs)

ETFs give investors the opportunity to invest in a portfolio of green companies—rather than individual ones—at a relatively low cost. Green ETFs specifically focus on socially responsible investing. This includes ESG (Environmental, Social, and Governance) ETFs, which invest in companies that excel in their environmental, social, and governance practices.

One of the advantages of green ETFs is the level of diversification they provide. Investing in these funds can give you exposure to a wide range of green companies across different sectors around the globe, significantly complementing your green investing strategy. Some popular green sectors include renewable energy, recycling, and electric cars.

5.5. How to Start Your Green Investing Journey

Starting your journey towards making greener investments doesn't have to be confusing or overwhelming. A good starting point is to do your own research. Understanding what makes an investment "green" is crucial. Use financial service websites, reliable news sources and public reports to understand the ethical, social, and environmental practices of the businesses you're considering.

Consider seeking advice from a financial advisor who specializes in ESG investing. They can offer personalized advice based on your financial circumstances and preferences.

Investing in green funds, rather than individual stocks, is a viable strategy for beginners, as it offers instant diversification.

Remember that while green investing can potentially offer financial returns, there is also a risk involved, as with all types of investing. Therefore, it's crucial to maintain a balanced portfolio and review it regularly.

By integrating green investments into your financial strategy, you can aim for robust returns while also contributing to a healthier, more sustainable planet. Make the conscious choice to combat climate change with your finance - make your money work for the planet!

Chapter 6. Saving for Sustainability: A Guide to Ethical Savings

Saving for sustainability is a fantastic way to help ensure a better future for our world, all while growing your personal finances. By considering the ethical implications of your savings and investments, you can not only benefit financially but also contribute towards a sustainable and environmentally friendly financial ecosystem.

6.1. Setting the Scene: The Importance of Sustainable Savings

In the past, the world of finance and the drive towards sustainability were seen as entirely separate entities. However, in recent years, a shift has taken place. This shift is the result of the increasing understanding of the interconnectivity between financial systems and the world's ecology.

Sustainable savings involve considering not just the financial return of your investments but also their environmental, social, and governance (ESG) impacts. This means taking into account companies' operational practices in relation to environmental conservation, social equity, and sound governance. By culling your financial backing towards organizations that adhere to these principles, you cast a vote for a sustainable future with each pound, dollar or euro saved and invested.

6.2. Understanding ESG Investing

ESG investing is the practice of integrating these environmental, social, and corporate governance considerations into investment decisions. Rather than solely focusing on financial return, ESG investing encourages the allocation of capital towards companies that follow sustainable practices, thereby fostering a healthier planet and society.

Every investment in a company that prioritizes sustainable practices is a step toward a more sustainable world. Furthermore, underscoring the importance of these investments, several studies have indicated that ethical, ESG-centric companies often outperform their less sustainable counterparts in the long run, proving that ethical savings can be fiscally prudent as well.

6.3. The Mechanics of Sustainable Savings

Initiating your journey towards sustainable savings is a process that involves several key steps. First, it's crucial to identify your personal financial goals. This could be saving for retirement, a down payment on a house, a child's education, or simply building a robust emergency fund.

Once your goals are clear, consider how you can align these with sustainable investment options. Research is paramount at this stage - understand the companies, look at their ESG scores and ascertain whether their long-term goals align with yours. Fortunately, there are several tools available today that provide ESG ratings for companies, making it easier to make informed, environmentally conscious decisions about where to invest your money.

6.4. Choosing the Right Sustainable Savings Account

Not all savings accounts are created equal, especially when it comes to sustainable savings. Look for sustainable banks or credit unions that use depositor's money to fund projects with positive environmental or social outcomes. Often, these institutions are certified as B Corps or are part of the Global Alliance for Banking on Values (GABV), providing reassurance that they abide by ethical practices.

6.5. Greening Your Retirement Savings

Your retirement savings can also contribute to a sustainable future. Consider targeting green 401(k) options or sustainable IRA's, which invest your retirement funds in a selection of environmentally friendly companies. Alternatively, think about moving your pension to a sustainable fund. These funds channel investments into green projects such as renewable energy or sustainable agriculture, providing you with a healthy financial future and planet.

6.6. Crowdfunding and Peer-to-Peer Lending

Crowdfunding and Peer-to-Peer lending platforms offer exciting opportunities for sustainable savings. By investing in projects that directly promote sustainability and ethical practices, not only can you expect a return on your investment, but your money will also help to foster positive social and environmental change. Research the platform thoroughly to ensure its credibility before you invest.

6.7. Journey Towards Sustainability: One Investment at a Time

Taking steps towards sustainable savings doesn't necessitate drastic changes all at once. Even small changes in your investment strategy can have significant environmental impacts over time. Start by gradually incorporating ESG investments into your portfolio or by switching to a sustainable savings account, thereby contributing towards the bigger goal of a sustainable future.

In conclusion, sustainable savings is about more than just financial security—it's about ensuring the longevity and health of our planet too. By contemplating the ethical implications of your savings and investments, you can have a direct influence on the kind of world we build for future generations.

Embarking on the path of sustainable savings doesn't just make you a savvy saver; it transforms you into an advocate for a greener, fairer, and more sustainable world. So, take charge, do your research, make meaningful choices, and watch your investments work a dual magic – beefing up your financial health and our planet's well-being.

Chapter 7. Debt and Sustainability: Managing Your Borrowings the Green Way

Life can be knotty when it comes to managing your finances, especially debt. However, integrating sustainability can create new growth avenues, helping you optimize borrowings in an environmentally friendly way. Today, we delve into the green approach to managing your debts.

7.1. The Green Lending Landscape

Green finance refers to the application of financial products in a way that promotes sustainability. Green loans come into play in this respect. Essentially, green loans are given to those who want to invest in sustainable endeavors, whether it be for eco-friendly residential projects or businesses seeking to limit their carbon footprints.

A winning feature of many green loans is that they often have lower interest rates than traditional loans because they are less risky. This is due to the fact that green projects typically involve innovative, forward-thinking strategies that are more resilient and adaptive to shifting environmental needs, making them less risky for lenders.

Moreover, the burgeoning market of green bonds, which are used to directly finance environmental projects, has opened up another feasible path for managing your debt sustainably. Green bonds are linked with lower default risks, hence, attracting a diverse pool of investors.

7.2. Budgeting Sustainably

Your journey towards greening your debt begins with sustainable budgeting. Managing your budget responsibly and in line with sustainable practices can help reduce your borrowings.

Consider creating an eco-friendly budget, a budget that prioritizes spending on green products and consciously reduces consumption. By paring down, reusing and recycling, you're not just protecting the environment, but also safeguarding your wallet. For instance, growing your own food can drastically cut back grocery bills, while choosing to cycle or walk over driving can reduce transportation costs.

Still, it's vital to be practical. Your green budget should be possible, not just ideologically appealing. Challenge yourself to sustainably cut costs, but remember to do so mindfully, ensuring you're not compromising on your basic needs or overall well-being.

7.3. Banking Green

Look to partner with banks who prioritize eco-friendly practices. Several banks are shifting towards green initiatives that encompass reduced paper usage with online banking, clean energy for their operations, and sustainability-oriented loans and services. Before opting for a loan, investigate where the funding comes from and whether it supports any industries detrimental to the environment.

7.4. Home Mortgages and Green Renovations

An often-untapped opportunity lies in sustainable housing. Many conventional banks offer "green mortgages" or energy-efficient loans geared for those looking to incorporate green renovations in their homes.

Green mortgages typically account for the savings gleaned from energy-efficient houses into the mortgage itself. By doing green renovations and cutting on energy costs, one can get larger loans with the same income. Besides, you'll also be helping out the environment by reducing your energy consumption.

7.5. Student and Personal Loans

Educational loans pose significant debt for many. Here too, you can ensure your borrowings align with sustainability. Some financial institutions offer green student loans with lower interest rates for courses focused on sustainability or environmental sciences.

Equally, when considering personal loans, you may want to explore green loans offered by various banks. Intended to fund eco-friendly purchases, these typically come with a relatively lower interest rate.

7.6. Credit Cards

Credit cards can be a source of significant debt. However, many financial providers offer green credit cards that contribute a portion of your spending to environmental non-profits. The motive is to promote sustainable practices and reduce carbon footprints.

7.7. Green Debt Consolidation

When debt becomes unmanageable, a debt consolidation loan can be an effective strategy. It involves taking out a single loan to pay off multiple debts, ideally saving money by securing a lower interest rate.

Luckily, green options exist for this too! Opt for green consolidation loans to wipe off multiple debts. Additionally, it promotes green living, reaffirming your commitment to sustainability.

7.8. The Balanced Approach

While managing your borrowings the green way is an admirable pursuit, remember, not all green loans are not created equal. Always ensure your borrowings align with your personal financial condition and don't forget to check the credibility of the institution you're partnering with.

Remember, the ultimate aim is to manage your financial affairs in a way that doesn't compromise your financial health or the planet. The power to create a sustainable financial future lies in your hands. Just as the small steps in your daily life make a big difference to the environment, tiny shifts in your financial dealings can drum up a big change in your personal finance world. Go on, sow seeds for a green, debt-free future - both for you and the planet!

This should serve as your comprehensive guide to managing your borrowings the green way. While it may require additional effort and shift in outlook, the pay-offs are certainly worthwhile. In the end, sustainability is not just an addition to our lives, but a prerequisite for a balanced existence on this planet. And you'd be contributing to that balance while keeping your finances sorted. It's time your money learned to speak green too!

Chapter 8. Retirement Planning: A Sustainable Approach for Your Golden Years

Retirement is not the end of the road - it's just the beginning of an open highway. Creating an eco-friendly, sustainable retirement plan will not only secure your financial future, but will also contribute to preserving the world for future generations. Like every journey, you need a roadmap to tread the path of sustainability with prudence to ensure fruitful returns during your golden years.

8.1. Understanding the Concept of Green Retirement

The basic principle of green retirement revolves around the idea of amalgamating your financial plans with environmentally-friendly practices. Instead of traditional investment instruments, green retirement encourages investment in vehicles that adhere to sustainable and ethical practices. The funds are channeled towards renewable energy projects, organic farming, green construction, and companies that endorse clean technology, carbon offsets, and environment-friendly principles.

Choosing green retirement doesn't mean sacrificing returns. In fact, an analysis by MSCI showed that environmentally focused indices have often outperformed their counterparts over the last ten years. Simply put, green investments are good investments.

8.2. Steps to a Green Retirement Plan

Building a green retirement plan involves much more than selecting the right investment vehicle. It's a comprehensive approach requiring careful planning, regular monitoring, and astute decision-making.

1. Listing out your retirement goals: Knowing what you want to achieve post-retirement will form the basis of your green retirement plan. It could be anything from sustainable home-living to setting up a small organic farm or a renewable energy agency.

2. Doing your due diligence: Not all that glitters is gold or, in this case, green. Some companies claim to follow sustainable practices on paper but don't deliver in reality. Research thoroughly about companies, mutual funds, ETFs, and bonds before making any investment decision.

3. Choosing the right investment mix: Depending upon your risk appetite and return expectations, ideal green retirement investment portfolio might comprise of green bonds, mutual funds focusing on ESG (Environmental, Social, and Governance) factors, and stocks of companies employing sustainable practices.

4. Keeping track of investments: Revisit your portfolio frequently and ensure that your investments are not diverted towards ventures that do not align with your green objectives.

8.3. Turning Your Home Into a Sustainable Living Space

Turning your home into a sustainable living space post-retirement can multiply your savings while reducing your carbon footprint.

Investing in solar panels, rainwater harvesting systems, energy-efficient appliances, a vegetable garden, and green building materials can help you live a sustainable lifestyle.

8.4. Green Lifestyle Choices for a Sustainable Retirement

Retirement is the perfect time to embrace green living to the fullest. Adopting sustainable lifestyle habits, from driving electric vehicles to reducing waste, investing in renewable energy, and promoting organic farming, can make a substantial difference.

8.5. Planning for Medical Care and End-of-Life

Healthcare is the most significant expense for most retirees. Invest in health insurance plans that prompt hospitals to reduce their carbon emissions and follow green norms. Even senior living communities today promote sustainability with initiatives like recycling and community gardening.

Meanwhile, planning for end-of-life may seem bleak, but it's an important aspect of retirement planning. Even here, you can stick to your sustainable living principles by choosing a green burial or donating your organs and remains for medical research.

8.6. Incorporating Philanthropy in Your Retirement Plan

Consider leaving a green legacy by incorporating philanthropy in your retirement plan. Donating money or resources to causes that further sustainability or contributing towards establishing green scholarships can have a lasting impact.

Afresh viewpoints and groundbreaking solutions are the keys to successfully merging your financial planning with sustainability goals, creating a green retirement that is rich not only in monetary terms, but also in terms of contribution to the planet. The path towards a green retirement might require extra efforts; however, the array of benefits it carries for you, your community, and the planet makes it all worthwhile. Your retirement years are an opportunity to relax – now, you can do so knowing your investments are doing their bit to preserve the world for future generations.

Chapter 9. Fostering Financial Literacy: Equipping the Next Generation with Green Money Management Skills

Financial literacy is an essential aspect of day-to-day living, and in an ever-evolving economy, it has never been more important for individuals to understand the financial marketplace and how to manage their personal finances effectively. But with the emergence of sustainable finance, there is a dire need to equip the next generation with the knowledge, skills, and attitudes about green money management.

Just like reading, writing, or arithmetic, financial literacy is a crucial skill—it has a direct impact on the quality of life, allowing one to navigate through economic ups and downs, make informed decisions and plan for a financially secure future. This holds particularly true for the concept of sustainable finance, where making informed decisions not only impacts one's personal finances but also the health of our planet.

9.1. Building an Understanding of Green Finance

Understanding green finance begins with learning about 'traditional' finance and then how that applies to sustainability. Like regular stocks, green stocks represent ownership in publicly traded companies. But these are not just any companies. Green stocks represent companies that are committed to environmental sustainability and renewable energy.

Your introduction to green finance needs to place a strong emphasis on understanding what makes a company 'green.' Evaluating a company's green credentials can involve analyzing various factors, such as the company's energy use, waste production, natural resource conservation, and treatment of animals. The company's direct contributions to clean air, clean water, and other aspects of a thriving planet are also worth consideration.

9.2. Learning How to Invest in Green Finance

There are a number of ways to invest in green finance, including green stocks, green bonds, mutual funds, and exchange-traded funds (ETFs) that focus on green investments. Mutual funds and ETFs can be a good option for those new to investing in green finance as they provide diversification.

Before you make any investment, it's important to do your homework. Research is essential in green investing just like traditional investing. This may include looking at a company's financial performance, strategy, risk factors, management team, and how compliant they are with environmental, social, and governance (ESG) standards.

One important thing to note about investing in green finance is that while it can be profitable, it should be approached as a long-term strategy. For example, while alternative energy companies may not currently generate the same level of profit as traditional energy companies, expectations are high for the future given the increasing importance of renewable energy.

9.3. Empowering the Next Generation through Green Finance Education

Financial knowledge doesn't always lead to action. But when individuals believe they can make a difference, they are likely to change their behavior. So teaching the next generation about green finance isn't enough. They must also be inspired to act.

To empower the next generation, financial literacy should emphasize achievable, realistic actions. By understanding that small, everyday actions can have a significant impact, learners are likely to feel empowered around financial decisions. For example, demonstrating the benefit of starting to invest early, no matter how small, can inspire young people to take action.

9.4. Measuring Success in Green Finance Literacy

Success in financial literacy, and in particular green finance literacy, is about more than just knowledge acquisition. It is about changing attitudes and behaviors, improving the financial wellbeing of individuals, and ultimately contributing to economic prosperity and sustainability.

There are many ways to measure success in green finance literacy, including: increased awareness and understanding of green finance concepts; improved attitudes towards green finance; changes in behavior, such as increased saving or investing; and outcomes, such as improved financial wellbeing.

Bridging financial literacy and the concept of sustainability can lead the next generation towards a path of conscious spending, saving, and investing, thereby helping protect our environment without compromising on their financial goals. As families, educators, and policymakers, it is our responsibility to ensure that our next generation is empowered not only with the financial skills they need to succeed, but also with a deep-rooted respect for the planet and a commitment to its preservation through wise financial practices - thus translating the concept of "Green Money Management" into reality.

Chapter 10. Incorporating Sustainability in Personal Financial Risk Management

In the realm of personal finance, risk management is central. It involves assessing potential risks and making decisions accordingly to ensure financial security. When considering sustainability, however, the perspective changes and the process becomes multifaceted. Let us delve deeper into how we can integrate these two important aspects.

10.1. Assessing Your Current Financial Picture

Before you can integrate sustainability into your personal financial risk management strategies, it's crucial to first have a clear understanding of your existing financial situation. Begin by breaking down your income and expenditure, assets and liabilities, and your saving and investment habits. This assessment will provide a strong foundation to build sustainable strategies upon.

Identify areas where you can cut back on expenses or increase your savings. This will not only improve your financial stability but will also provide additional funds that you could direct towards green investments. Pay close attention to your debt as well. Aim to pay off high-interest debt first, allowing room for sustainable investments.

10.2. Sustainable Spending Habits

A big part of incorporating sustainability in personal financial risk management revolves around making sustainable buying decisions.

These often indirectly affect your finances by saving costs in the long run and minimize the risk of straining resources.

To start, consider eco-friendly alternatives in your purchasing habits. This may involve supporting businesses that prioritize sustainability, opting for products made with recycled or biodegradable materials, or reducing your energy use by buying energy-efficient appliances.

Various other aspects can also be streamlined - from water-saving plumbing to solar energy systems and sustainable gardening or farming practices. These practices can result in savings over time, reducing your overall financial risk.

10.3. Green Investments

Instead of traditional investments, you could consider investments with environmental, social, and governance (ESG) factors. Green or sustainable investments focus on supporting businesses and projects that are committed to sustainability. This way, you reduce the environmental footprint of your financial activities, while also often achieving competitive returns.

When selecting investment options, scrutinize the ESG ratings of companies or funds. These ratings typically assess companies' environmental impact, human rights records, and corruption levels. In recent years, several ESG-themed funds and green bonds have outperformed traditional investments, precisely because sustainability often translates into better risk management and future-proof business practices.

10.4. Insurance and Sustainability

Insurance plays a considerable role in personal financial risk management. It is more than just a protective measure against unexpected perils. When aligned with sustainability, insurance can play a part in promoting a greener lifestyle.

Consider insurance companies that reward sustainable living. Some insurance firms offer lower premiums or other benefits to customers who lead eco-friendly lifestyles, have energy-efficient homes, or use electric cars. Utilizing such green insurance plans can reduce the financial burden and contribute to a sustainable future.

10.5. Taking Advantage of Government Policies and Initiatives

Governments worldwide are increasingly encouraging sustainable practices among citizens and businesses. Grants, subsidized loans, and tax benefits are some of the ways your government may encourage investments in renewable energy projects or energy-efficient appliances.

Keep yourself informed about these policies and take advantage of any that align with your financial plans. These incentives can significantly reduce the risk associated with your personal finances while promoting sustainability.

Options like green savings bonds are emerging as attractive sustainable investments. They are low-risk securities that fund projects with environmental benefits.

10.6. Sustainable Retirement Plans

Yes, even your retirement planning can incorporate elements of sustainability. Pension funds with ESG considerations can be favorable for an eco-friendly way of life and places your retirement savings in businesses that prioritize sustainability.

Check with your retirement plan provider about sustainable investment options. Some providers offer a range of green funds.

Switching to a sustainable retirement plan doesn't just ensure your future income is sourced responsibly, but also that it reflects your commitment to sustainability.

In conclusion, sustainability does not need to be a stand-alone effort, detached from other aspects of your life. With some guidance and focused intent, it can be organically integrated into your personal financial risk management strategies. Understand the effects of your financial habits on the environment and on society. Making the switch to sustainable practices helps not only conserve our planet but also opens avenues for financial security and prosperity. And remember, every small step in the right direction contributes to the larger goal of sustainability.

Chapter 11. Bringing It All Together: A Comprehensive Check-list for a Green Financial Makeover

Today's personal finance journey must not only be economically wise but environmentally conscious as well. This thought is especially relevant as we are all tweaking our lifestyles for a greener tomorrow. Now, let's delve into the comprehensive check-list which will guide you to a green financial makeover, step by step.

11.1. Understanding Your Current Financial Situation

To start with, take a good look at your present financial situation. Analyze your inflow and outflow of money, your assets and liabilities. Consider the following points:

1. Assess monthly income and expenditure: How much are you earning and how are your earnings spent?

2. Examine your debts: How much do you owe, and what are the interest rates?

3. Analyze your savings: What are your short-term and long-term savings plans?

4. Determine your investments: What assets do you own (stocks, bonds, mutual funds, etc.) and what is their current market value?

5. Plan your insurance: Do you have adequate insurance to cover various risks?

The above analysis will help you comprehend your overall fiscal standing and form a base for green financial planning.

11.2. Shifting Towards Green Investments and Spending Habits

Once you understand your financial picture, it's time to identify your environmental footprint in it. Understand where your money is being invested and spent and if it has any ecological implications. Determine how it can be redirected towards more sustainable and green-focused areas. Consider the following points:

1. Divest from non-green investments: Analyze your investments if there is any involvement in fossil fuels or any other non-sustainable industries.

2. Redirect your investments: Instead, select green-friendly companies or sectors dedicated to renewable energy, sustainable practices, recycling, or conservation.

3. Control your expenditures: Align your expenses towards more sustainable, ethical, and green products and services.

11.3. Establishing a Green Savings Plan

In addition to green investments, you should also establish a green savings plan. Here's how:

1. Set saving goals: Ascertain how much you want to save and for what purpose (retirement, vacation, emergency fund, etc.).

2. Savings medium: Decide how you want to save that money (regular savings account, high-yield savings account, bonds, etc.).

3. Green aspect: Make sure the medium you choose for saving

favors sustainable practices.

11.4. Aligning Your Debt Management Plan with Eco-Friendly Practices

Consider your current debts and how you plan to repay them. Redesign this plan to align it with sustainable practices. For example:

1. Green loans: Opt for debt instruments that have a lower carbon footprint like green loans or bonds.

2. Efficient repayment plan: Aim at paying your debts earlier and save on interest, which in turn reduces the money footprint.

11.5. Evaluating Your Insurance Needs

Insurances are a critical part of any financial plan. When evaluating your insurance, consider the following points:

1. Insurance type: Examine if the type of insurance you have is supportive of green practices. For example, some insurance companies prefer electric cars over traditional cars.

2. Coverage: Find out if your insurance coverage includes sustainable replacements. For instance, if your home was damaged, would your insurance support rebuilding in a more sustainable way?

11.6. Educating Yourself

Lastly, continue your education in green finance. Financial markets and instruments continually evolve, and so do environmental standards. It's vital to stay up-to-date on green financial practices and adopt them wherever possible.

This comprehensive check-list isn't just about having a green financial makeover. It's about evolving your thought process and viewing your personal finance from a fresh, eco-friendly viewpoint. The crux lies in understanding the symbiosis between your financial health and the planet's health and implementing practices that cater to both. The road to becoming a green investor is a journey. It might require a shift in mindset, but it's a journey worth embarking upon for a financially and environmentally secure future.